Romer

ALSO BY ROBERT EASTWOOD

Snare (Broadstone Books, 2016)
Night of the Moth, Chapbook (Small Poetry Press, 2007)
Welkin Gate, Chapbook (Small Poetry Press, 2003)
Over Plainsong, Chapbook (Small Poetry Press, 2001)

Romer

Robert Eastwood

Etruscan Press

Etruscan Press
Wilkes University
84 West South Street
Wilkes-Barre, PA 18766
(570) 408-4546

WILKES UNIVERSITY

www.etruscanpress.org

Published 2018 by Etruscan Press
Printed in the United States of America
Cover design by Laurie Powers
Cover painting: *Spaceship* by Aron Wiesenfeld
Interior design and typesetting by James Dissette
The text of this book is set in Sabon.
First Edition

17 18 19 20 5 4 3 2 1

Library of Congress Cataloguing-in-Publication Data

Names: Eastwood, Robert, author.
Title: Romer / Robert Eastwood.
Description: Wilkes-Barre, PA: Etruscan Press, [2017] | Includes
    bibliographical references.
Identifiers: LCCN 2017033265 | ISBN 9780997745580 (softcover)
Classification: LCC PS3605.A865 A6 2017 | DDC 811/.6--dc23
LC record available at https://lccn.loc.gov/2017033265

Please turn to the back of this book for a list of the sustaining
    funders of Etruscan Press.

This book is printed on recycled, acid-free paper.

*For our children, Elaine, Glenna, Callum, and Craig, and,
as always, for my wife Dorothy. They are my company of loves.*

"It is unimaginably hard to do this—to live consciously, adultly, day in and day out."

—David Foster Wallace: Kenyon College Commencement Speech, Delivered May 21, 2005

TABLE OF CONTENTS

Romer

I

Foothills

The intellect is like a small boat, afloat in history.

"...while looking all around, endeavoring
to understand new things."

—Dante's *Purgatorio*, Canto II, lines 53-54
(Mark Musa translation)

Canto I - From Waters

For better waters, now, the little bark...

You turn round in mid-life, as did a Florentine,
enter a forest of confusion,
              then go from darkness to open blue.

You reach a shore with all your
              offenses, rare loves & losses,
failed hopes. You assume a slow atonement.

This is Romer, an earnest striver,
              a stumbler through his days,
whose life is a riddle.

It began here. At the foot of that mountain,
at the watery verge of breath, Romer floated.
              Warm, aqueous jelly.

Currents held him plumb in this liquid world.
              So, much later, when he walked into
the seducing sea he felt, as immersion grew,

an enticing, yet fearful, return. Then as depth
              & press increased, a palpable awareness:
he was not made for a liquid world.

If he sank below he would die.
Yet, at once lightened, he could shove against
              the sea's salty aspic,

repel the constant pull & pressure.
              He moved with the sea into a marvel
of unremitting breath. The sea, the waves of his heart.
                            *

"I saw the opening maw of hell / Arched over me
a dismal gloom, / While all God's sun-lit waves
rolled by, / And left me deepening down to doom."

To Romer, the deeps are analogous
to mystery, to a millennia of dreams, & beasts
within depths, human beta-versions.

If he could see the huge heart inside a whale,
he'd know a room with four chambers, where,
head up, a child could step through valves

large as a saloon's swinging doors.
He can see, though, the pelicans,
strung in endless thought, perhaps a dream,

a journey pelicans envision as they skim
the flooding shore in their concerted scan
of stretched-foam-shallows. Down their

pocketed snouts they read the sea, its screed
of ancient tales, for the one melodrama
whose finish sustains them. Romer thinks,

It's all so serious—even a mussel's gristle
has earnestness, a determined grip on shore's
certainty. Shrouded in fog, grave intentions

stay within quiet coves. Currents wash & draw,
boneless creatures drift, jointed old & new,
the birthing scrum bends with ebb & neap.

Of the real heart of the largest beast
we know little—what inspires a creature
of one hundred feet?—nor do we really know

the slighted flow that birthed us, blurred ebb
& neap, the froth-tatted water seen roiling,
unrolling at our feet. It's a well of excretion,

yet to Romer there are principalities
in its depths, whose emissaries, intent, practiced,
glide between our toes. Blood's

archetypal recipe, amorphous brine,
shake of salt on our bitten tongues. Why look
from provenance toward shore? Why build

outposts on sand? Could be, we tire
of pull on our balance, the clumsy way
sea wants us. Its graceless spray puts us off.

CANTO II - WHICH ROAD IS BEST

The sun was touching the horizon now...

No Master coaches him, his years pass
                in negligence. The mountain rises up
                before him, he has no recognition.

One early year, a summer spent in measles welts.
His bedroom walls blistered
                like his skin. Come September,

he left fevers & junior high's hormonal
                chaos to become a freshman
                wandering halls on shaken legs,

bumping beefier kids. Girls he'd left
                last spring slipped past like swans.
Everywhere size tormented.

His dick, minuscule in the P.E. shower,
                his paltry arms, ridiculous. The rooms
                echoed with significant words

                he couldn't understand. The gymnasium
rope he must climb stretched into shadows,
thick & ominous.

He wished for weekends, his work for a gardener
                with grimy knots for knuckles. A small,
vine-thin man, leathered brown as a boot.

Call me Manfred, he'd said, & gave Romer five bucks
                a day to push a mower, edge crabgrass,
                pull spurge weed. Manfred's truck's

doors half-latched with the thin clatter
of trashcan lids. Yellowed windows would not
wind down. The seat, taped-over cotton spillage.

A boggy mat covered floorboards where
        marigolds & petunias rooted.
Hired with a handshake, Romer rolled his sleeves

        on hairless arms, Brylcreamed his hair, worried
        who he was & wasn't.
Manfred's overalls hung empty about his hips—

so happy with so little—the glory as he chewed
        his cheese sandwich, beamed after he'd had a pee.
Romer liked the shrug when

        clients avoided them. Some, wraith-like, peeked
        from dingy curtains—left requests
        on screen doors, or stashed notes under porch rocks.

Romer discovered grand, far away sweetness
        in new-mown grass. Yard by yard that year
        he rooted gorse & loam, trimmed

        scruff to small, observed disregarded grace.
He searched for *his* way in the sun.
His muscles taut, his mind wandering.

*

1.

What of work, tasks of muscle & nerve?
Romer took work as it came,
tried his hand making & rearranging.

Canto III - His Own Shadow

In sudden flight those souls were scattering...

Ideas, it's said, emerge from looking
at something a while & seeing
something else. Suppose, Romer thought,

you could take your private self, what you
greet in the dark, pin it like a photo on a wall
beside someone else, someone

special. Would that worthy person,
that idol, show you, in contrast,
how you should rearrange your life?

Flying in a Cessna upstate, Romer had such
thoughts of Thoreau. His warped reflection
in the pilot's dark glasses stirred ponds.

A loon, a solitary loon, emerged from rushes.
They left grey surrounds
of La Guardia. Below, autumn gold,

epaulets of green. The Lycoming
rose an octave, revved to higher
altitude. Possibly Henry heard

a loon's lyrics each evening at his pond,
& wrote the music out in syllables
with a pencil he'd made of cedar—

paper he'd folded from a sack of nails.
Maybe his stoop's rough plane warped
letters into Greek of his Harvard texts,

or curled them into strings of quarter notes.
Such evenings ant armies ran campaigns,
owls dropped cloaks on mice.

Macadam veins below cut fields & hills.
Cars, alien as lice. Pines must have
rustled atop their dark shins, light

from a farmer's window sputtered on the surface
of the pond. Maybe Henry thought of the acres
he'd tindered cooking fish in a stump,

the foolish lunch with a comrade. As the plane
droned on, Romer felt sunken in his world,
at odds with mysteries. So many *whys?*

Henry's work was botany-balderdash
to some, who saw him a strange hypocrite.
Around smoky hearths, they heated grease

for gravy, spit out his name. Did Henry
hear voices, like loons' evening songs,
he could never understand?

Canto IV - Interest Of The Heart

When any of our senses is aroused...

They had found a pension, Romer & his wife,
in a back alley behind Toledo's
ancient walls.

The nodding owner hadn't shaved in days,
looked haggard from drink
in his faded beret.

Romer lugged their bags upstairs,
a dripping toilet,
a bed. A single bulb dangled above.

In the night his heart freewheeled wild.
No effort would
slow its pounding ever faster,

as if on open throttle. Romer paced,
woke his wife. He feared bursting
like an egg, running red & gooey

down the stairs onto Toledo's
blackened cobbles.
She said, calm yourself, lay back down,

go to sleep. She turned while he bounced
at the foot of the bed,
spun like a dervish.

He feared his chest ungluing.
El Greco's stretched faces stared in corners,
ashen & severe, a sheen of green

on the walls.
The place was strange. Panic
pounded in his nose & squeezed his eyes.

Babble from his mouth, silly pops,
the arc of wild humping—
a gang of German students through the wall,

bedsprings a counterpoint—he pulled
the light's chain, his wife sat up, opened her
quilted wings so he curled down, laid his

cheek on her breast—soft, softened by her
slow heartbeat—he thought,
I am no Cid.

                              *

          Romer saw reflections without mirrors.
There were the nearest, the loves, & those
distant, like Benny, from whom he learned.

The Benny Romer knew never outgrew
his professors' mustiness, those inversions
& tropisms of a would-be Henry James.

Even on the phone Benny spoke
in a mandarin, hortatory style, unafraid
of sounding phony. Toxins alarmed him,

Benny brooded about his food.
Took lots of pills, lots of water
kept him pissing. Made excuses, forever

nursed maladies, griped of a day's misfortunes,
hid at times in his twin bed, the same room—
Benny & his ma—not a normal fellow.

       Romer's girl then was a nurse.
When introduced, Benny stuck out his limp hand.
Later she told Romer it was like holding

an old man's pecker. He never knew an uglier guy—
short, waxy, balding—even at 25—like weeds,
hair on his temples, stubbly, thin & wiry,

no eyebrows, his eyes had a lizard's bulge
& the chin he had, tucked under liverish lips.
Romer thought Benny hated being a Jew.

       There were so many reasons to despair.
His family left Austria pre-Anschluss,
made it to China, wound up as prisoners;

just a boy, he remembered the soldier's grunt,
the satin slide of the sword & his father's
placid head, the open eyes. But Benny died

nobly. A neighbor kid he didn't know
chased a ball into the street & Benny
jumped up, unfurled wings he'd hidden—

Romer never knew. Picked up the kid
& dropped him safe in a hedge,
but the Cadillac's alien fin

did him in, clipped him,
so he spun head first into a tree.
Old lady driver thought he was an angel.

CANTO V - SHE SAID REMEMBER ME

...already parted from those shades...

      Romer had his Beatrice, at least
as a vision, borne when her image
pressed into him like a signet seal.

When Romer first saw her
in a North Truro parking lot,
the kids bickered behind him, the wife

sought knick-knacks while he bided
in the car, the radio playing,
You're So Vain, & people parked,

arose from their mobile shells
like amazed hatchlings come
to term—he passed the time

imagining the better lives they led—
it was '72 & he was underway
        on summer holiday.

      She appeared in the bed
of a battered pickup with a Labrador
which bounded down after the driver

squealed the Ford to stop,
tossing her against the cab—
she laughed—her hazel hair held

from her face by a flowery garland
across her brow—hair fanned across
her shoulders, over the faded granny

15

lifting her breast from out
the elastic tube, while Romer's wife,
as is her habit, gazed off listening

in the din of crowded voices
to an adjacent conversation—
this time between two blue-headed

women rambling about buying
gifts for those back home,
& the absurd cost of clothes.

No one but Romer beheld this girl
who had come again through tangle of years.
This time Romer

would catch her eye & nod, he wanted her
to see it was him—that he was kindred—
                then he shied, shuffled on to be underway.

CANTO VI - A REPLAY

The loser when a game of dice breaks up...

He saw a time in his childhood
when guessing the moves of others began,
his playing intricate games.

Romer climbed over years & was seven,
when second grade seemed so complicated,
& all the others so *in on* the mystery,

why they joined there at Joaquin
Miller Elementary. Unlike him, they knew what
to say to Mrs. Vary when she raised

her eyes off the page as Dick & Jane skipped
after Spot (that quadra-pedal, ever-
romping imp), or when she stood, quizzically

suspending her all-knowing & angel-
white chalk. That searing angel-whiteness!
He thought now of death, as the mountain

arose before him each morning,
but not then, not when sport of war played out,
silently, in *funny* papers—rifles

with POW! shouted in capitals, as if
labeled for the deaf, the orange splotches
bursting at barrels' end, asymmetric

flowers of noise. Wounds kissed off, bombs
danced between, bullets sidestepped as they
zipped across the frame trailing easy-seen

lines. At school, luminous girls,
especially Pia Simpson, her braids glistening
as they coiled down her back,

knotted by bows he longed to touch.
He'd draw chase-scene-comics of Pia
& himself, laid them on her oaken desk.

He'd pencil parallel lines & snaky dots
he'd decided were lyrics.
In his comics, with the entirely good

& completely bad (those fought beside
or fought against), she appeared, her hair
feathered, simply dressed,

never the circlet Swastika on her arm,
or in Dragon Lady black, but a clingy dress,
polka dots, wartime khaki, or a blouse

& skirt, torn, barely covering.
She always helped, this comics girl he loved,
running with him away from bad guys,

holding his hand as they scrambled into airplanes,
or jumped from roof to roof, clamored
impossible crags, his gaze at an angle

so a hand or arm thrust out of a page,
caught onto speed in the still movement
of a cartoon box, as if time itself

could be pieced out in thrilling, frozen
instants, where the awe of living,
in sublime silence, burst from pencil & paper.

She'd see he wasn't just the boy who reddened
having peed his corduroys
on teacher's reading rug.

*

Marble games matched
his hunger for winning, what with his
willing thumb, his determined aim.

They knelt away from the odd boy.
The boy saying he was
barefoot because of rheumatic fever.

Beside the steamy walls
outside their school galley,
breath delighted them in wisps

through orange morning sun.
Ignoring the boy's shiver, they drew
their ample circles—as the girls squatted,

scooped their jacks, hopped or stood
like herons over chalked pools,
squealing at their proper distance—

while boys thumbed their agates,
peeking up from Bull Durham bags,
learning the glassy eye

they would use someday at poker.
Knuckling their steelies that cracked & sent
goodies across the line.

Romer saw how far
they seemed outside the circles,
the girls, as if boys

drew a more serious world
with only themselves inside, as if they
would always prevail in the game of taking.

Canto VII - It Is—It Cannot Be

When this glad, ceremonious embrace...

Romer had a birthmark on his back when he was young
                shaped like an arrowhead.
He told his friends it was a scar passed

to him somehow by a skirmishing
forebear. He told his friends he was part
                Blackfoot. Such marks for them were common,

he told them, a hereditary trait,
                he said, in redskins. He told his friends
many foolish things to explain who

he really was, or would be. He hated it
in the mirror, stuck over his scapula
                like a sign, *Go Directly To Jail,*

like a *Turn Here For Jesus,* like
                the direction to God knows where, beyond
where he could ever go. Then one year

it wasn't there—he thought the year
his daughter had her breakdown, or perhaps
                before, when Bobby Kennedy sprawled

in the Coconut Grove. No. He remembered
                the certainty it wasn't there when his father
died in Rupert, Idaho, when the breathing

became a chain dragged across the floor,
clattered down in a coarse sigh.
                Romer had sat beside the bed

all that night, hating wanting it finished,
     sick of sterile walls, the gasps of pumps.
Afterwards he went home,

he switched on the lights,
turned about in the nakedness of his
     red skin, where he bled.

        *

Romer watched his dad skewer each rear leg
onto a spike—pierced at a fleshy apex behind the joint.
The carcass hung like an empty sack.

The knife, with its grey hone darkened by blood,
cut skin to bone around the legs,
as if grooving anklets.

There were slow drips of blood from the open mouth,
the rabbit's yellowed teeth. Unperturbed eyes
looked off into nothing.

The blade pushed inside each rear leg & cut
till it reached a junction at the groin, then
slit down the belly to the neck. With a twist,

it cut through to drop the splay-eared head.
His dad laid down the knife, pushed his fingers
into the groin, & slowly peeled off the pelt

like a tight shirt. Romer saw the coruscated body,
naked & meager—all but the forepaws, those imploring
dirty mittens. The knife gnawed

bone to sever them. The belly opened
its multicolored sacs & lumpy tubes,
which pulled loose

from filmy integuments. The heart, a dirty brown,
Romer remembered most, flesh like his own.
His dad's implacable palm.

Canto VIII - Coming Of Nachash

It was the hour when a sailor's thoughts...

Sailors once thought sea demons
were serpentine, beyond being knowable,
threats, enticing snakiness.

Serpents slithered ever after because one
gulled our foremother, when heritage hardened.
To serpents, loss of Eden was loss of legs,

a mutual enmity, instilled like the undue shame
that bodies harbor, the unending feud,
& too, mix of love & fear as sailors favor sea.

No dreams are planned. Do we really see or hear?
Are they fathomless ocean? In one Romer heard
the Nachash speak. *My purported subtlety*, he said,

just hyperbole, though, I do enjoy
this little repartee we're having—the exception—
an arbor tête á tête with those string-haired nudes—

I refer you of course to that rib-sprung wench
& her hapless, so dupable dude—
they've made my perambulation slithery.

I myself dismissed the good or bad
of apples, but what a fateful bite that was.
She craved the core it seemed.

This so-called enmity of ours began
with a curse, & feuding's botched our blood.
Look, if humans really knew—understood

as to my bent...er, to be coldly frank,
I am by nature unctuous, expressly now,
in this belly-dance I do—yet trials,

prostrations, haven't rattled me—
but yet, it's true, I've been much maligned,
mercilessly, as if I'd outdone

Belial (an assignation over
apples surely palls beside millennia
he's promoted ruin, all things undone).

There might be cause to run
if I were really what you humans think, if it
were more than wising up some clueless

rubes about the world & its delights
that brought all this, my tonguing dust—
how sad it seems—& I should know—

to damn us all, as if either could
avoid his passion, what sort we be.
You see, I dream in this dreary hole

for rapprochement, a hoped likelihood,
or if your lot saw me, well & good.
But all you see is metaphor

for treachery & guile. To me
you're implacable, across a breach
I vainly coil & twist to swing.

You have a blinding grudge, resolved
to instinct now, aimed so to shun
all offers of a peace—a détente

with my sort awaits a single wink,
any sign, tolerance might've begun,
& yet you won't, not one.

Canto IX - Keys To Seeing

Now, pale upon the eastern balcony...

On a steeper path, the terrain altered
as he looked back, as memories
of ignorance sharpened.

Everything comes to a point. Why did it take
so long to see that? Brunelleschi raised
his hand & pointed toward that dot where

everything meets as if it was a great sump
of light sucking sight to infinity.
That was after centuries of the uniform

plane, oblivious of the third dimension.
Marcia's drawings in third grade had a slant
toward an A+ Romer's never did.

He stood behind a painter once who put
a daub on the middle of her canvas.
She called it the navel of her picture,

where it all begins & ends she said.
Romer didn't get it then. As a teen
he worked as a laborer one summer.

He carried stone for masons in a hod.
The plan for the building was paper-flat
& tiresome on a table, like the scaffolding

he climbed to dump his stone
at the mason's feet, but in the Supe's hut
Romer also saw a drawing

that had one corner of the building pinched,
distant from the front corner & wall,
like Marcia's did, & the building arrived

in his mind in that squeeze toward vanishing.
It wasn't just a dead bed of straight lines
& angles, it was alive in what he

saw as reality. That summer too
he'd pretended to be sick. He was truly sick
of the labor & the mugginess, so he

let his boss down, snuck to the movies.
Romer watched his first 3-D picture,
a hot Kansas City matinee,

& the theater floor was sticky with
spilt coke & smelled like belched popcorn.
Behind cardboard glasses he saw *The House*

of Wax with Vincent Price, & he ducked
a paddleball & other kitschy stuff,
& the near & far of perspective

again came to him, magically,
out of a blur of edges. It took him
so long, & he still peered at perspective,

at how many he'd disappointed or fooled
with his selfishness, at the way it all
was covered over in his mind, & then

about what his grandpa had told him
a long time ago...it's how you look
at the vanishing point. In the end everything

is a gag, or so said Charlie Chaplin.
Romer realized he was symmetrical one day.
What he loved could be divided, then folded

so the outline became congruent.
He appreciated amorphousness,
it was so often beautiful: the warp

of a bristlecone, the puff of a cloud,
the concavities of a stone. But where
was shape's balanced conformity?

Then he discovered words like himself—
like his body of symmetrical
things. These letter-bodies also made

sounds that were symmetrical.
If he were Bob, the name would begin & end
in the same place. The Greeks saw in this sort

of word the movement of crabs. We all
string words, backwards or forwards.
Not only could words be symmetrical,

symmetry often hedged meaning,
much as did Romer with his lies.
He found these nice curvaceous words

could have antithetical senses.
Take gag for instance. Many splits, like a clump
of mandrake roots. Gag could be to stifle & play

a stunt, to plug & to pun, to block &
to wisecrack, to check & to joke. You can
gag on the gag some guy pulls, or play

a gag by causing someone to gag.
Antipodes, set at odds. Once Romer saw
a *Star Trek* episode where people were

split down the middle, one side black, the other
white. Some black on the left, white on the right,
& others being just the opposite.

They hated one another. Symmetry
is a point of view, a way to fool, at time aslant,
where balance is but a fleeting glance.

II

Midlands

"…Take comfort, for I see I must
perform my duty, now, before I leave….
—Dante's *Purgatorio*, Canto X, lines 91-92
(Mark Musa translation)

"Because you make things of this world your goal,
which are diminished as each shares in them,
Envy pumps hard the bellows for your sighs."
—Dante's *Purgatorio*, Canto XV, lines 49-51
(Mark Musa translation)

CANTO X - THE HUMILITY IN DUTY

When we had passed the threshold of the gate...

Security & justice, pat excuses for duty.
        What if duty goaded your daemon,
the urge behind urge, pushing you forward?

Duty's initial hurdles are little nuisances:
        like parking in a red-curb town,
the security search, your belt, your keys,

your phone & watch, all your metal
piled hurriedly in a plastic wash-tub
        to traverse a furnace

of Superman-scoping; & the gloat
        of dun-clothed deputies, as you re-gather
your dignity & find the diminutive arrows

to where numbers will be winnowed.
Judgment day, the dutiful herding toward
        some oracular pronouncement,

carrying out a duty hoped to be evaded,
        or at least deferred into a nebulous future.
Romer brought a book. He found people more interesting.

He scanned the room for the biggest breasts
(a foible imbedded in his amygdala).
        He spotted a 5 on a scale of 10 across the room:

her hair coarse, hominy gold,
        her tight, Perry Ellis jeans almost
cleaved her in two. Yet, hefty knockers.

One guy ranted on & on with his blue-tooth,
as if all must care about his botched delivery.
        Romer liked the fellow with whiskers reading Kant,

& the Christmas sock a mousy woman knitted.
        After three hours, & two visits to the john
(where graffiti focused on duty's boredom),

a mini–skirted maven of the law minced
to the podium (the same lady who had switched on,
        earlier, a video describing honor & privilege

of jury duty, complete with common folk
        who read in monotone the rote
from cue cards at forty-five degrees)

& announced that all of the cases today
had been plea-bargained, & regrettably,
        they could all go home. The mousy one, with an

awesome knitting-needle lunge, spiked her way
        first in the rout to the door. Romer jostled Breasty.
It was afternoon. Not far to the Sweet Tree Bar.

Besides, Breasty led him up the block.
Sweet gum spiny pods littered the way,
                making a black slough to tread between.

The barman's tattooed arms semaphored
                as he dipped smudged glasses into suds
then circumscribed each brim

with a clockwise twist of his grey rag.
The drinkers stared at this,
                as if it disclosed tricks of the craft,

or could this be a clever charade
        they've been called by duty to deliberate?
Romer counted many deliberative drinkers in his

forebears, ready to make it duty to decipher
whatever this fog-covered world gave glimpse of.
        He was not sympathetic with duty

any more. Let someone else have a crack.
        In the bar, it was a ruckus of inner turbulence.
Nobody talked about politics or the weather.

Too much going on inside.
Romer asked if anyone had read about the manatees,
        how the gentle souls were dying

& nobody knew why.
        The barman said, what's new?
Why does *anything* that hurts *nobody*

have to suffer? *Guys give me lots of business*
trying to figure that one out, he said.
        It usually comes to them after four drinks.

Blake's Urizen with his calipers on the bar's wall.
        Where prophets dwell, Romer listens
& performs his duty, just as he would pity.

Canto XI - Empty Glory

"Our Father Who in Heaven dost abide..."

                  Where in history do you awaken, alive, wanting
      order in the world, though deception gloats in the mirror,
           an implacable Caesar reclines in the sky?

             Back when you were taught to use the biographical index
      in the school library, when Cords still cruised streets, stopped by
semaphore stoplights, Romer squalled forth. The *appeasement interlude*

before the big war. He thrived, spent the duration wetting his bed.
Maybe you came later, when men were still expected to wear hats
& carry lighters. Maybe you watched the grey newsreels afterward

        of Jews bulldozed into pits, wondered how in the hell
            Jesus let that happen. Maybe you came later.
His was a boyhood fed by nickel matinees, Zane Greys, Buz Sawyer

flying sorties & the cartoon curves of his lovelies, Red Ryder
    with that thonged lever-action that never ran out of bullets,
Lash Larue's whip-cracks—ordinary days, when on the world's

other side, shit rained down. Maybe like him, you hate clouds,
kitchen-cabbage odors, maybe you too avoid bullies, but could easily
   be one. Things like that are common. In such an insulated life,

        is it strange he hates any loss?—like that Ingersoll that filled
with home-plate grit on a fruitless slide. For years he kept the tickless
thing. Maybe your parents fed you on the dreck of loss as well, filling

you on bile, making you lick your plate. In his case Christian Scientists
   prepped him after school, & for a while, he led on the Mormons.
He pictured theirs a fun, zombie-church when an 8th-grade cutie

averred her daddy baptized the dead. It's possible you dropped
all that in your secondhand paper bounds of Sartre, Camus & Kafka,
& maybe you avoided malleability & didn't fit into corporate life

like he did. But it was a feint for him, being Republican—some
pack instinct he felt, as well as greed & crass ambition, for which
he later atoned, voting LBJ & mailing a respectable check to MLK.

Oral Roberts cured him of serious religiosity, but maybe you,
just in case, pray nightly on your pillow. No matter how well
he thinks of himself, he's lapsed on honesty—with his flexible

fairway scores, his fictive gifts to March of Dimes. Maybe you
disagree with him, his denial that parents fuck you up.
(To you, perhaps, it's mutual.) If you were his friend you'd notice

Romer's grown deeper lately. He's seen that the Heimlich maneuver
doesn't always work. His uncle croaked on a plug of charred steak
he'd dished. Maybe you've caught up in seeing all it takes to die.

Canto XII - To Raise Your Head Again

Like oxen keeping step beneath their yoke...

> Years erode, skin sloughs.
> Hours pass in habitual ruts. Work, spent at necessity.
> Circles trudged over & over, a year-weighted yoke.

> Whatever it was, Romer would like the mojo he had at fourteen,
> when he'd scale trees, his shoulders & chest tingling, skin too tight,
> when he strutted home from fifty-cent movies, still hearing bugles

> of *Battle Cry,* & Aldo Ray's husky voice, buckled & buttoned
> in marine corps green, when he walked a be-anything world.
> Around the Korean armistice, they lived on L.A.'s 98th,

> & he walked distances, his blood pulsing in his fingertips.
> Across greasy concrete, the corner cycle shop, Royal Enfields &
> Nortons, the corral of Triumphs leaning on their legs, the tarry smell

> of lubricated metal, rubber's carbolic sweetness, & in the shop window,
> a romance in flames & golds on glossy posters. From school he'd
> always go to the little market, where, upstairs, his friend James

> the cripple lived. James' sisters sewed in corners of the room,
> a sour cabbage odor aged the air. His mother drying her hands
> on her skirt, bowing, James nodding in his wheelchair;

> his grandpa's recliner before the 12-inch Zenith, the old man
> swigging Kirin in a kimono; the tacky surface of the Nauga-
> hyde divan Romer'd sit on to tell stories for James to smile—

> tales which browned the lampshades. Up 98th was different,
> misted pylons, insulators ticking, clapboards squatting
> behind ice-plant, oleander, fry grease odors—

bacon, onions, potatoes. Nothing smelled as fine as 98th
between Main & Broadway. A DeSoto with spoked wheels—
the one old Wilks wanted running—sat like a scuttled barge

in the gutter; his son, Stanley, the boxer, sparred
on the front porch when he saw Romer, to say hello,
since he couldn't speak but in grunts & huffs. That's where

Romer had *his* first fight, in front of Stanley's house.
A black kid spit on Romer's shoe & his buddies cackled,
slapped their thighs. A priest skidded his Pontiac to make them

shake, Romer's nose bloody, the black kid spitting a tooth.
What a grin he had, that kid. His blood on Romer's knuckles.
He threw the bird when two nuns in the priest's car shook

their fingers at them, clucked like roiled hens. Romer
could still hear streetcar bells on Broadway, smell blue-steel-electric
stench of stops, so palpably, but he'd lost the sass of his mojo.

CANTO XIII - WAYS TO BE

Now we are standing on the highest step...

Stairs, steps with shadows, & shadows
of shadows, stairs always steeper,
insights opening as windows.

Romer's crape myrtle, his garden shed,
              wavered in the sun's slow course
                   past his window, as hues flickered

in a day's phases, as if time itself
              covered the canvas at which he looked,
                   revising it, like Monet's cathedral,

re-painted by Rouen's changing light.
Windows speak with silence, like a tree or cloud.
Through his idling car's windshield he has watched

a single file of quail quickstep march across the road,
& he recalled the opposite, the traipsing,
unmilitary lines of a junior high field trip, when,

in orneriness, he tugged Pia's pigtail.
              Her grin, digging a fingernail in his ribs....
                   Windows exist outside our human purposes.

Romer was that young Russian, shocked
when he saw his father through a window
flail the air, joyous, tossed aloft

by serfs; & he kept that flooding vision
beneath a pillow, to have it enter dreams
on lonely nights, when he floated,

untethered, above his failing father.
　　　　　　Windows open beyond surprise.
　　　　　　Romer smiled at a friend's fertile sleeplessness,

for through her bedroom window, from
polished darkness, she saw a tom-turkey,
strutting, puffing, preening, & she thought

of a honeymoon night, where she
& her love danced naked in the rain—
to hell with the world's dark windows!

Romer would be that husband whose wife's senility,
　　　　　　a sleep-walking vapor, crept past windows
　　　　　　of all their books; her striving for sense

sharpened by gouging a red pencil
　　　　　　under each word, tracing each line, scaffolding
　　　　　　paragraphs—a husband

who bought more books,
more pencils, who enabled hapless choices.
A window re-signifies the world.

　　　　　　　　　　　*

A friend who steps into forever
beyond knowing—betrays him,
leaves Romer behind & weakened.

Romer shook the man's hand, patted his shoulder,
but her sorry husband wasn't why he came.
Somewhere Over the Rainbow, by hum & ukulele,

hovered like wing-thrash above her casket.
A tripod placard had her name—but no.
Not for Romer. For him, her real name, from

a Chinese uncle, who, when she arrived, proclaimed her sex—
a *Grrr*. Thus a growl with an invisible vowel is what Romer knew.
A young usher, a stranger, had a brush-mustache;

must be her son's friend, or a functionary of the chapel.
He guided Romer to a folding chair & with a curt hand
signaled him to sit; like the *Savage* himself he seemed—

what she called her favorite painter, Gauguin.
Van Gogh & Gauguin—that was a pair—
Romer read about them in her coffee-table book.

They painted inverse worlds in adjacent rooms,
argued over whores & the way to care for brushes.
Vincent razored his ear, then, amazed,

struck off a commemorative painting.
Gauguin sailed to the South Seas, to laudanum land,
a tropical forgetting of what he did or didn't do.

Stargazer lilies & Old Spice gusted off
a creaky couple waddling down the aisle.
Palm fronds stirred at the chapel's window.

A constant sway, Romer thought, as in the Marquesas:
lazy palms & Gauguin's sloe-eyed, languorous girls,
who curled to him, unafraid of strangeness.

The uke played on as if dying deserved a hula.
Grrr knew now what death brought,
she played very well at the proprietary muteness—

that selfish silence of the *passed away*—finitude
spoken of timidly, in ignorance, on the precipice.
Another marker in Romer's reveries, a silly name

he held as if it were an amulet. Amidst bald pates
& candied curls, with Gauguin's shade, Romer's heart
beat on. Over the rainbow, rainbow, rainbow.

Canto XIV - Old Corruption

"Who is this roaming round our mountainside...?"

He walked with ghosts.
Not disguised, the shades lingering
from history, whose curious rubble remained.

At the Charnel House in Rouen
         Romer knew nothing was simple or clear.
You could tell him of trees, those in the middle

of the courtyard,
                   trees that waited & sought light.
The withered rosettes of grass.

A rood of steel & stone.
                   You could tell him of bones
that filled the ossuary.

Those filmy windows.
Carved skulls that emerged from wood,
         & scythes, & shovels, & the dance of skeletons.

Wood-grain has more allure than fear,
like the surface of sin.
A serious edifice, withered wood in half-timbered walls,

black as if charred. Blades chiseled across veins
                   in the beams, leaving leg bones,
ribs, phalanges of disease, fevers,

a dead forest so close to all.
Crowds look in dark windows sensing spirits that stare back.
　　　Tell them of the black cat behind glass,

the dry cords of skin.
Yet, when you speak of an atrium for the soulless
　　　you must pause for sun to strike dry timbers

at just that crux of light
that they are made beautiful,
& trees stretch, & in the macabre texture

of incised bones thrives, in faint laughter,
　　　　　a wry resignation,
a scene hung as backdrop, not a curtain.

　　　　　　　*

When cancer came Romer wanted it gouged out.
He hired a company of performers,
skilled in their lines & scripted motions.

With others, rostered into numbered, curtained
cubicles of faded green, pervasive in that place.
Apportioned to their spaces, those on the playbill

& their audience, crowded between gurneys
covered in washed out green & white.
Bustling shoulders nudged the curtains,

urgent readying, with bundles of pale green.
Tubes & masks dangled, instruments to probe
about bare necks. A kit was brought,

toasted, whey-green blankets, clothes discarded
for a wispy gown, a green leaf over nakedness.
An Asian woman across the way surrounded

by her chanting family, she supine, a quiet Buddha
on the green, engulfing bed.
Voices everywhere but no faces,

each celled unit awaited its call behind the cloth.
Into each tent the assigned professionals collected,
probing before entering with scrubbed fingers,

introducing themselves as if on a set of green curtains
for wallpaper, & the gurneys, paisley love seats.
Setting about preliminaries, explaining

features of near death, procedures taken,
what to expect as momentum of the act began.
Nervous laughter at an awkwardness, glib immodesty,

the pale green bonnet all must wear like a shower cap,
dangling strings over surprised skin.
Then the entry, the epidural twinge

& cold sweat at not moving, the green pallor passing.
Onto the gurney after a jab for veins, closed cold
& wincing, taped with a tap & intravenous well,

wheeled away through spreading doors
into a cold room whose lights
were great glass flowers with stainless

stamen. Onto a table tumbled,
center-shuffled, Romer was introduced
to the green-garbed, as if at a party.

Some pretty faces busy before they masked,
centered him as a target, more green cloth
piled upon him. The loving voice that said

it's time, the cone that wavered before his eyes,
as if to give its silent kiss, secretly.....
This, but a stage in the exodus.

CANTO XV - OPPOSITE OF WRATH

The same amount of time it takes that sphere...

Sun that vibrates skin, that pulls
at the pulse & ripens skin...even the blind
know its light & the shape of it.

Besides making love Romer needed to walk,
said the doctor, so he sauntered in the park
to forget his heart. Ahead, under sycamores,

she smoothed her hair
like a teen reveling at the touch of it. Perhaps a bee
she'd flicked away? She dropped her brush

into a market cart heaped with plastic bags.
When she turned—a ruddiness, a painted grin,
more gum than teeth—Romer saw one hand held scissors,

the other, a newspaper page. She laid them
in the cart, no, on a black plastic bag.
A ritual began, sequencing invisible things,

waving a pencil, placing strings.
Romer felt the sun as it threaded
the sycamores. Breezes shirred

the leaves—everywhere, dapples.
Spare some change, mister? With an index
drilling her cheek, she bent her knee,

one varicosed leg out-stretched to curtsy.
Lacing the cart's basket-wires, paper dolls
with crayoned faces, each a unique posture.

Light danced on her theater
of tissue bodies. The bags bubbled like tar
in the agitated, irresolute sun.

For a buck she offered Romer a paper doll
made of newsprint, this odd woman.
He walked on

with a body, a face, without smudge.
A chest, committed to his palm, throbbed
at the wobble of his thumb.

The shuddering leaves, the whole
mysterious way into which he walked
into his heartbeat.

Canto XVI - Our Tendencies

The gloom of Hell or of a night bereft...

        Low & dense came aftermath.
The air crisp, drunk with oxygen.
Delicate lace across the ruin.

It's a willow land, a creek bed
on a dawn after the storm,
& as Romer's boots grew heavy

in the coiled grasses,
gorged with wetness,
he remembered, strangely,

his little cousin,
so many years ago, born a blue baby,
& his uncle picking up

the little body,
the almost translucent skin,
stark against the pressed shirt

his uncle wore for Easter.
How his uncle's gnarled,
carpenter's fingers

gently brushed the thin wisps of hair
from little Earl's pale forehead,
the blue eyes burning through.

*

The rutted trail in Bort Meadow meanders clover,
cow dung, a few squat oaks, then joins a path
rising to a grove of Eucalyptus.

52

The trees seem stunned, caught with flensed bark
about naked shanks. So many variations
exist of blue gums.

These are eighty feet, & at the sky they leaf
on branches thinner than a man's thigh.
When Romer walked through Bort Meadow

he felt like a ragman, picking up
in his *mind's eye* what he saw, no matter
how it may have been ignored,

thought unimportant, used-up, or broken.
He made labels in the transaction from eye to mind—
he notched air for what he saw, open to words.

He could not stare at the sun,
but sunlight on any latent thing
pulled him like someone pointing.

Over the surrounding hills were freeways & crowds,
yet he heard only trees in Bort Meadow,
wind pushing them to yaw,

sheaths lapped by sap, complaining to move,
choiring, like bows drawn slow.
A bed of alyssum, a Scottish thistle, a blue jay,

a single poppy, a green rivulet below a root.
No reason for him not to ask—why was he there
with a basket of reason?

They hardly supported him, fragile words,
yet they were all he had for this or that.
He lapped one against another into a pattern.

He would make a bit of profit.
Romer juggled them for purpose he could salvage.
They let him think, they let him imagine somewhere

there was sovereignty. Many times below branches,
Romer would envision an empty swing, pushed by breeze,
& he wished for a solid body there.

Canto XVII - The Seed

Reader, if ever you have found yourself...

As his path continued, he averted
his face, but his father always followed,
in the broad emptiness of those winding

acres. Mountains are but legend in Idaho.
Does your father find you, too, in your
sleep, on a morning run, his face browned

like he'd spread out on some shore-cot,
or sat in the dirt-bake of homelessness?
Does he sometimes step from a picture,

his features almost your own? Maybe
you didn't raise your hands to close
his coffin, or rub your fingers on the oak's

grain. Without your words in that cold
sanctuary, his spectral image stays.
You stared too long into Idaho sun.

If you'd latched the gate, attended in those
last days to his preparations, he would
have found a hill in all the flatness,

without looking back & pulling.
You run & run on high-crowned Idaho
roads in your lightweight shoes beside

the stern, harrowed rows. Nowhere high enough
for God to speak. Oh, your rare blood keeps
as if everlasting. Before you there's

a flat horizon you will never reach,
you think, till you one day see it all
          as an ascent you climb, shedding skin.

        *

     Several years before he died
Romer's father broke a sand dollar
    on the flat back side,

    took the five, winged seeds
& glued the disc, face intact, to a plaque:
    winged shards, shredding teeth

    when alive, floating on wood
like bees about a flower.
    He'd found poetry of a sugary mood,

    & with brown indents
he singed edges of these verses—
    patina of timeworn parchments—

    the poem stuck with shellac
below the dollar. The year
    & his initials on the back,

    a chosen avatar.
Romer thought it a cloying relic.
    The poem declared the dollar

    a symbol, Christ's gift,
& the fragments mystical doves.
    How strange for his father, so adrift

& lone, impatient with dogma-peddlers,
pushing their fold-out tracts—
    hucksters he labeled *Holy Joers*.

    Yet, with time, a life turns within.
Inside his fingerprints, Romer saw
    scattered bits of a hope's underpin.

CANTO XVIII - CLOSE TO MIDNIGHT

When he had brought his lecture to an end...

       Tell me, what makes a life one's own,
for Romer's fingers spread to have it all,
but nothing held. An old man sums

his years, a child counts minutes.
Like a mockingbird Romer sang, perched
on ambition's spire, waited for sunrise.

Light on his face didn't hold. He danced,
reached boundaries where steps
had no purchase, showed a swagger.

Where do lost graces go? His body collaborated
with coarseness, his skin leathered, stropped
by time. He walked on feeble shins.

Romer's blood sought release, turned skin
a splotchy brown. Far away, a whimpering child
on his chest, poppy-chains edged a new-seeded lawn.

Breathless moments. July rain. Strolls along
a Como shore, shared champagne & Mozart chocolates.
He went on, but nothing held.

He thought of what he hated—how rot grows,
fire to ash, horrors he'd imagined
taking all he loved, cries in cold wards,

a child's early fate, slaughter for a gospel's
sake. The sybarites' zeal for sex in paradise.
Romer stared at the clock at midnight,

when icy light crept across the bed,
& sensed in shadows a presence unseen.
He waited for a day, or a night, of revelation.

Canto XIX - Siren

It was the hour when the heat of day...

      Deserts tempt with shimmering lakes
of wetness. The desert is false.
In hazy distances, promises betray.

Romer saw her in the row
      enveloped by smoke, one of those souls
that riveted him, his double on a blazing screen,

his sins laid bare.
Maybe it was the ropey vein on her temple
thumping a tempo of military zeal that says it all,

that says, *Fuck off, I'm winning, buster.*
      Maybe the grin she wore like an old Buick.
Maybe the angry, devil-be-damned intent.

What about this woman, what about this place,
about this Mecca of Tea Party piques,
      desert replicas of the Forum & Sphinx?

      It wasn't her oat-bucket handbag, her floral
mumu, nor the oxygen bottle she'd wheeled in
coupled to a pulsing, viscid tube,

dangling above her heart. Nor her Camel butts
smoldering like a dumpster fire.
Everyone smokes connected to some threat

they've wheeled to Vegas.
She kept jabbing the buttons, her yam-like
fingers had the intransigence of certainty.

She sat in a cornucopia of trills & bells,
marches, booms & toots unceasing—
the Kodacolor screen spinning

bananas & cherries, jokers & chevrons.
She ignored the washboard-thresh of banjos
        from the gazebo above the bar.

Let her be. Let her be amid the jack-
hammer din, for this was Las Vegas:
cavalier with ruin, dismissive of nuance.

Let her feed the electric maws
that are virgin to a knurled coin
but hum a tally on Led's under a smoky nimbus,

impersonal as drones—
        let her go until the game plays out
or she explodes, for it's all a show

ablaze in neon anyway, & shows must end.
It's a trailer length away from heaven,
the draw of greed, the revenge of Indians.

Canto XX - Feelings Spur Us On

The lesser will yields to the greater will...

Romer knew the pull. Half his life had passed
racing to win that spin, to raise his head
above the rest. When he worked in New York

the sore was reddest. He scratched it every day.
At lunch he walked about & saw desire's variation.
Today, no doubt caught on security cameras & pixilated

on God's gray screens, streams of women
        click down halls, issuing from portals
bermed with pewtered snow. Crowds cull

into doors as if they were drains.
Women press one another to elevators
        unmuffling chins swathed in damp wool.

        They tug gloves to unsheathe cell phones
& thumb tweets in private oblivion.
Hanging in the air outside this very spot

was an early Seventies summer noon
where Romer'd buy a dog & kraut at a steaming cart,
then take a walk past Wall to Nassau,

bumped shoulders with occasional braless girls
        who giggled as they jiggled past, arm in arm,
exuberant at being pretty.

Across the narrowness of crowded, greasy cobble,
an open-air shop teemed with women who picked
& pushed with brassiness they'd had to learn.

Dark men stretched with glistening arms to grab bills
over Jersey lettuce, string beans & dirty potatoes,
        over tipped crates. Their stringy hair,

torn, sweat-splotched tees. Butts gnarled their faces.
The men shouted a Basque patois to one another
& at the women in puffed bouffants, cinched

dresses, free of input-output trays,
Steelcase desks—milling, elbowing, shoving.
To Romer they crowded inside a common mind,

        women of different times, lovely as they thronged.
While men, taught of herds, railed at a world of sorry
repetition, women strove to glean & find the good.

Canto XXI - As With Solid Things

The natural thirst which nothing satisfies…

Care—which has ravelings Will would tidy
through sleep—was dry thirst for Romer,
& sleep an oasis with water's sweetness.

Romer woke the night his friend died,
at the same time, & tried to sleep again
through imagining he was cast away,

making a bamboo shelter on an island
where he must survive—hut-building,
diverting in challenge & response from

bleaker thoughts: flitting fingertips on frets.
Of course Romer was unaware
his effort at sleep was in synchrony with death.

When he trenched the boundary of a hovel
with a fantasy half-coconut, furrowed
a berm in a rain-whim verging to sleep,

she went under, her heart stopping.
Eighty-three years old, & she had lived strong.
A month-long coasting down & down,

threading tunnels of serious depth,
refusing ardent church ladies, who carried
consolation like collection plates.

When Romer was ten, a half-built church stood
around the corner from home: a short budget
left open wall studs, imposingly tall,

with zinc-coated tunnels below joists
for hot or cold conditioning. Boys crawled
these ducts as they snaked up, down & around.

They scuttled, their ways turning into a labyrinth.
Romer & his friends played weekends, no workmen.
Their noises echoed in the incomplete soul

of a serious plan that meant nothing but fun.
That soon-to-be serious building,
intended for magnitude, where death & birth

& serious thoughts were to be honored, meant nothing.
They scrambled within the half-timbered crux
of significance, heedless, happy, just boys,

acting with untroubled energy.
Why do delight & dole so often wed
about the voracious drain?

CANTO XXII - FALSE ASSUMPTIONS

By now we had already left behind...

yet he still saw his dad shake a finger, tamp each word
in Romer's ear: You pay money, you get a damned receipt!
It had taken five bucks to buy Owen Phelps' bike,

yet Owen's father banged on their front door & said
Romer had stolen it—Owen, grinned from the car,
the little weaselly bastard.

Romer had turned open an old album he found
in his folk's attic. It had pulpy black pages,
sepia pictures held by little triangular pockets.

In one, his mom wore a fur boa, her eyebrows
drawn in arcs, a style of Thirties movie stars.
She held his crimped face, a busted-bud wrapped

in bunting, out for view, a well-earned prize
for nine month's work. White wisps diffused
about her lips. Borealis of happiness

made by winter air. That's when it dropped,
a square of browned paper—a receipt for *Services*,
St. Mary's Hospital letterhead. So simple

compared to modern computer spill: *Ten days,*
thirty-seven-fifty, Care of Baby at five dollars,
& Circum (an ironic short cut in red), *two-fifty.*

Total, forty-five dollars, net, two-fifty, after forty-two-
fifty paid on admittance. A pass to go home,
bundled, larval, eyes bleared, vague as to use.

Dollar signs swirled in a broad-nibbed Thirties'
respect for hard-earned gelt. Beside the spattered
Olds his dad must have decided, *Get out the Kodak*—

un-bonded as Romer was, thrust squealing with timbre
that seemed so tentative—& who in God's name
could tell with hospitals?

Canto XXIII - Old Poets

While I peered up through that green foliage...

Romer met a poet who was soon to die.
Her fourteen-line poems, like leaves in autumn,
settled on musty shelves & forgotten.

Though her root's been cut, her children
still hear her count feet, thump lines
on the kitchen table's oilcloth.

She learned to write sonnets one rainy day
after she'd spanked her daughter
for teasing. Her son had wet his bed.

She took a blunt pencil & sought relief from
yowl & din in rhyming & iambic rhythm.
Her mind loved the order of sonnets.

The volta with the shock of winter sun.
The painterly accuracy of rhyme.
The gut-satisfaction of an ending couplet.

Her friends, the old poets, know the body
follows a willful arc, reverses its reach
one day to a slow curl from the sun.

But they believe as well
that poems breathe as live offspring,
they have an iron-sluice of blood.

Some poets die young, some live to see
their beloveds go before them.
Some watch their dogs take the circle

to death with cavernous eyes, a dun silence—
the quiet way God answers us—embodying
the unsayable each poet would want to write.

Her friends gave tribute at her dying—
garments cinched, soft genitals snugged,
toes growing cold—a hum, ice-like,

constant in their ears. A true company,
which cherished holy meld, its unlikely
weld of petals & dough.

Canto XXIV - Poem's Process

Talking did not slow down our walk...

They talked past one another, the poets,
as if moving at different speeds, into & out
of different worlds, where words were cries.

Celia's honey-black, refugee skin,
her soft convexities—so *ripe.*
She nervously laced one red-tipped finger

in her hair as she read, curling a ringlet,
again & again, as if she coiled a wisp of air.
Celia (who modeled to support herself

& her child) wrote incessantly
about the ineradicable lien on an artist
who cornered her as she dressed

after a figure-drawing class.
She spread herself down a wall
in mispronounced words

in soft Cuban singsong—about a dream,
ripped underwear, crying in a dark corner.
The group grunted as they usually did,

a shallow approbation when any poem
is finished. Her grammar was atrocious.
As for bad dreams, they tend to feature

desperation, & Celia's strove
for consolation after rifts in dream territory.
That could work well, or not, in a poem.

Then Sue said, *In my dreams, it's not*
intentional as well. Yet I'm so blatant—
I want to hide my cleavage, but I can't,

I'm a lure of pressed-togetherness.
That's my scary place...my tits verge an abyss.
Celia murmured, *si, si.* Again they grunted.

A pinch of flesh makes a different kind
of nightmare—a trap by being female.
Night lets go (as they did) with a shrug

when dreams end, & you open cautious eyes
to a world settled into parallels of light
on all the safe things you've left about you.

The group made no comment on Celia's poem,
ignored her eyes pulling at their faces.
Don't tell but show, written on the wall.

*

The army is no place for poetry,
except in words squeezed off from triggers
& pain, out of diminishing self.

It was a clumsy poem, scrawled
on the back of an army mimeo—
He'd written it, Romer remembered,

in Sarge's tent, waiting for an ambulance—
his left arm in quarter-sized blisters
throbbed of poison oak.

Sarge had tried to scrub it away with GI soap.
A literal pain in the ass, the poison oak,
it invaded their bivouacs subversively.

A whole ward existed for it at Fort Ord.
Guys got it taking a crap,
having a smoke, leaning on a tree.

Sarge's wife found the poem in a drawer
        after he died,
& Romer's address on the Internet.

He'd been a son-of-bitch, one of many
        sergeants they'd hated that summer.
Any time someone farted they'd say,

Sergeant who? He'd called Romer
a piss-ant soldier, said his heart may belong
to Jesus, but he had a collar on Romer's ass.

Said college boys marched
        like knock-kneed girls—
the usual non-com trash talk.

Romer read somewhere Lorca heard a whore
singing on *Callejón Tóxico,*
or Poison Alley. At first he thought

        it was a cat, an estrous yowl,
then he realized those trilled words
        were from a forgotten poem,

one he'd given his martinet of a teacher
        as a way to say he was more
than good for nothing.

Canto XXV - Form Of Our Desire

Now was the time to climb without delay...

An old saw: act on what you believe,
        for the fog is thick, & no one
really knows a goddamned thing.

Given the world's plight, Romer thought
everyone must know this—as in dogs
        have half a soul,

as in the day to buy gasoline
        is Monday,
as in children who crush snails,

wringing their hands,
grow into Francophiles
        or arch conservatives,

as in Nero's favorite color
        was green, & that he
dressed in it, demanded peas

& leeks, & at the games
wore laurel leaves not as tradition,
        but out of love for verdigris,

as in millions of black men
        aren't really missing, aren't swept
down a sump of the state,

or spread like grease on ghetto avenues,
        as in the common political game
is perplexity, like the quandary

posed by Hobson, in whose livery
one had the choice of the horse
　　　in a stall nearest the door,

or no horse at all, beyond protest,
　　　just as with Henry Ford,
that scrooge of color,

who pitched his Model T
to a speed-starved populace.
　　　We must, as we skate solid ice

in company with our shadows,
　　　sun above our shiny faces,
feet toasty in our socks,

trust the glue of certainty,
as in what we glide upon stays firm,
　　　as in what shivers below stays murk.

Canto XXVI - Shelter

While we were walking at the ledge's edge...

Rain & threat pair equally
        as you tread where choices spread,
on a path that perversely narrows.

Weeks & rain had not abated,
        as if stubborn gods resisted correction,
as if, like feckless Mayans, we needed

heart's blood for placation.
Between showers, at a dry doorway,
        Romer watched a preacher tucked

into sandwich boards painted primitively
        in Bible verses. He stood obdurate
in the downpour, a drenched rooster

declaiming water's ruin & salvation.
Passers lifted blasé chins—the preacher, another
        irritant in the slog back to work.

Angry-prophet-eyes followed the doomed souls
        quick-stepping down a doused sidewalk
to escape, & shouts came ever louder.

Rain obeys its nature. We make the misery.
        Skip the caterwaul evangelism.
Maybe say our fat is mostly water,

assert gravity's pull, atomic weight,
that sinless rain seeks ditches to flood.
        Rain carried away Romer's

mother, sure in her latter-year mania
	she was a naughty girl again.
Romer's favorite evocations: water's breath,

how it takes on wipers' heartbeat—
rain-blurry gray, odors of mohair, sweat,
	rolling wet in the backseat of a Chevrolet;

the unfair constraint of his grade 4 classroom
	with crabby Mrs. Crawford's snapping fingers,
a clock ticking, tear-streamed windows.

Later, rain's crazed fingertips drummed
	at his office's seventh floor window,
far above the preacher in his scrimshawed boards.

It drip-stippled the sill, finally paused.
Below, in pools on every tar-pit roof,
	worlds of windows about to open.

*

Times that are the shits, when nothing
seems to square with what should be,
when your best intentions go limp.

The final lap, you're thinking all may be going well,
when a guy with massive quads ices your sweat.
That's '71. That's *Me and Bobby McGee*. ICBM's.

Polyester leisure suits. Tricky Dick & Viet Nam.
An interloper, a scab, Romer walked through
Greenwich Village on a national strike of AT&T—

always running into surprise—as if today bled,
like a watercolor margin, into a strange tomorrow.
The very first day, a soft, pink fellow in a kimono

led Romer into an apartment papered in a collage
of penises. Romer must *repair his instrument*, he said,
sotto voce. His walls resembled paintings

of faces emerging out of carrots, turnips
& celery stalks—except these tedious walls
writhed of wilted cattails & pale pears.

Once Romer knelt to twist his screwdriver while bodies,
serenely naked, surrounded him in Klieg-light heat,
the fretting porn director in Speedos, a Kiss tee.

Ah, the virginal relief of dial tone.
Romer climbed into the Chelsea Hotel to repair phones.
Dylan T. bellowed in the walls. Romer spliced wire

on tenement roofs, tarred & torn, aging in the sun.
He gave a few bucks to a grunge, cheeks mossed
of grime & blood, crouched in the piss-radiance

of brownstone stairs. Romer hid his beneficence
on company vouchers—till he saw his derelict
gunning a cop car. Nights, Romer would sink under

enormous towers, built to last forever, they said,
into the PATH tube's dingy light & arm-pit air,
to emerge, older than expected, on a Jersey cloud.

III

Upper Reaches

"What is a life? A frenzy. What is life?
A shadow, an illusion, and a sham.
The greatest good is small; all life, it seems
is just a dream, and even dreams are dreams."
—Calderon de la Barca, *Life is a Dream*

"...an old man, by himself,
who moved in his own dream, his face inspired."
—Dante's *Purgatorio,* Canto XXIX, lines 143-144
(Mark Musa translation)

Canto XXVII - Joy Is In Reflection

It was the hour the sun's first rays shine down…

It seemed a paradise in pastel the morning
Romer strode through customs & he was
welcomed with a stamped *bienvenido.*

A week in Cancún, & Romer lounged
in rooms with the pervasive smell of mold.
He felt askew as the walks' terrazzo.

Beveled faces, beaked profiles, temple glyphs.
Birdlike, children cried, *¡Hola, hola!*
¿Dinero? They grinned & clawed

as silent women prodded their backs.
Hotel Fiesta Americana, *réplica pirámide,*
rose, scaled with scaffolds—brown men

climbed in a mélange of time,
their paint verged unstuccoed lath,
they brushed murals before the frame was whole.

Sagas of sacrifice could not wait, serpents writhed
among them. In their *hora de almuerzo* hombres
leapt through cilantro scent, wore plumes

& painted leather. Above, they aimed
for great stone lobes, their rackets roared
in the streets like treed jaguars.

As they ate tortillas, shots caromed
from afar, hard rubber balls
concatenated in the heat—they chewed on reverie.

They played in paradisiacal temples.
The bikinied blonde sidled a conch seller,
his pink-lipped shells echeloned on the sand.

At first she bartered, then suspended
her white arm in the sun,
lifted the shell to bleat loud wails.

She twirled in heedless jubilation.
The seller withdrew beneath his fronds, & he watched.
At mildewed covings others swept

polished tile, others raked hairy seaweed
over beaches, opened doors, scrubbed steps.
They listened, unseen, their eyes scudded.

At day's end they crowded Dino buses
amid tarry smoke, returned to
white-washed huts on a plain

of leaves & mottled lime.
On the aquamarine horizon,
over the Isla de Mujeres, a squall formed,

a sail like Joseph's coat billowed against
the gray sheen of distant rain.
Cruelty in midst of beauty dismayed him.

*

The sun seemed to melt the ubiquitous green.
She dressed to undress, & he had more
appetite than could be slaked.

Me gusta mucho, she said,
sucking fingers that scooped Romer's salsa.
Cilantro hovered

in the thickened light, as on that plain
before Kukulcán, when they ran
from rain, found a stele

inscribed of Mayan war. Romer's fingers
traced plumes that folded like
tropic leaves around profiles

& hunched backs. Her fingertips toyed
at filed teeth. Sun slashed through
a crevice, surprising them. The steep,

lichened stages to the slab
where victims suffered,
& in the tiered, moldered steps

water pooled. Silence
but for rain—yet awake, clamorous
with cilantro & mold,

odors hefty & spacious. Garlic,
onions, tomatoes,
lime, a nip of jalapeño—

oh, yes, leafed cilantro—
they make a bloody mush to corn-
spoon from the bowl. She grinned.

Her clawing fingers beguiled him.
Romer wanted to lick them.
Salsa clears the sinus, lovey—

frees body-smell, that
gorgeous jaguar with liquid,
carnal pacing. You see within

the skin the meat of appetite.
At the Sacred Cenote she
pointed at a metate

that lay beneath a banyan's
reptilian roots, its black,
pebbly face long flushed of meal—

a cenotaph, she said,
to the gut. Their guide described
a sacred book, where gods

fashioned corn into men, steeped them
in lime. When Mayans ate
flayed warriors they were only corn,

you see, transfigured. They kissed
& chewed the chips. She leaned into him.
Bloody salsa burns my lips...

*

Life's blood is so close to the skin there.
Lick its salt in the very air,
touching only your body's heat.

Romer saw a silent lagoon,
an amethyst plate pushing the horizon,
& his eyes watered from the brine

as it precipitated in berm-bounded pools.
Rows of white sacks like monstrous larvae,
set in hive-like order, geometric,

& the workers crawling, hoisting, running,
the ground a mix of pepper & salt.
Romer saw huts under thatch

where women waited with babies,
silently watching what he watched—
in the opaline heat, air saline sharp,

muscular little men in shorts & baseball caps,
backs stippled in crystals, running barefoot
up a narrow ramp into the semi-truck

with 75-kilo sacks in the clutch of neck & shoulder.
If one should slip off the ramp he would die,
Romer thought, the sack's weight snapping his neck,

yet each had a carriage, proud as he labored
before his woman. They all knew their burdened
running, hefting bags heavier than themselves,

involved by its feint with risk a reason to be men.
Silence was an aspect of their focus.
Nothing grew near this soup of sodium

so like blood, its traces embedded
in tusks of wooly mammoths, trees,
bones of cavemen, in sources for ancient wars.

Such crystal irony. Romer could sweat for them,
watch them glisten in their menial work
indifferent to the heat.

They ran because pesos were for piece work,
another rubric given the poor,
& they had no way to spend his respect.

Canto XXVIII - A Place New To Each

Now eager to explore on every side...

Van Gogh's Provence was misery,
yet Eden in art he produced.
Romer had reached a country of beauty.

When tossed bits of baguette, the woman's Jack Russell
      snapped at the bounty as if famished.
As she drew on her Gaulois, sipped her Côtes

de Provence, the dog's eyes tracked each move.
A widow, perhaps, sharing a brasserie lunch
      with her dog. So magnanimous, the French, with dogs,

just as they absolve the detriment of physical flaws:
Sartre's cocked eye, De Gaulle's nose, Lautrec's demi-legs—
then there's St. Denis, the patron saint of Paris,

who walked, headless, six miles, preaching all the way.
Romer watched the dog at lunch in a brasserie in St.-Remy,
& later, on that summer evening,

he found a concert at the Chapelle Saint Roch
on the edge of town, built to honor a man
who beat the plague...by dog.

(As Roch lay banished in the thicketed wilds
the saint-yet-to-be's sores were healed by a cur,
which licked them with a miraculous tongue.)

A string quartet played in the chancel, & behind
in the apse, Saint Roch himself lifted his marble
skirt in a pose Colbert employed in *It Happened*

One Night—but *his* thigh held the bite of stigmata.
Telemann, Vivaldi & Haydn. The bassist—
well-used—an oily-haired worldliness men have

in French movies—pumped to Vivaldi's spry tempos.
His nose had a sizeable, glowing wen, but who
cared, as he, with élan, led the seven other players.

The second violinist, a young woman, swayed
on stilettos, her eyes fixed on the leader's rosy nose.
She frenziedly see-sawed till her poor bow frayed.

An old Labrador snored in the narthex beneath
the ticket seller's chair, ignored like a minor saint
posing in the dark recess of a cathedral niche.

Canto XXIX - A Painted Flow

Then, like a lady moved by love, she sang...

There are complexities in songs of love,
there are tonal colors, bittersweet pigments.
How do you apprehend the crafty depths?

      Romer stands at the Manet, watches people
stare, then drift by, in the way the pensive
walk past art—proprietarily, as if *he* had painted,

had composed, wished to share the meanings.
      On the marble bar—a bowl of oranges, a rose
cresting the rim of a glass, & champagne,

green, glistening in gold-caped bottles.
      Heavily, she leans on the bar & stares.
      She's tired, & smoke burns her eyes.

Lamps flicker. His chapeau gleams as he
mumbles for a drink. She strains to hear
over the uproar, the undulant crowd—

it's an instant's apprehension.
      At the center, while all about her flows
a welter, she faces him, enduring,

the hint of tension in her face softens
to veiled entreaty—though what shows
      on the marble bar—a bowl of oranges, a rose,

chiaroscuro bottles—glitters in a gaiety
she tends to, she shares nothing there.
An oblique mirror behind reveals that

we—*we* are the man who mumbles,
who holds the girl in his gaze as she leans
          toward us, awaiting, through the skein

of her sense, the wish we present her.
Or, could what seems a simple meeting
at a theater bar—the roses not germane,

cresting the rim of a glass, & champagne
          unstoppered, be more complex,
with her weary stance before us,

her palms pressed down, as if to lift
the heavy marble counter, to topple
it all, the bottles, the cut-glass bowl—

could her tension suggest repulsion?
With that, Romer saw her look:
exasperation, there, about the eyes?

Though there are oranges, cordials,
          green, glistening in gold-caped bottles,
          serving—restoring—they play no part.

It seems she's not inclined to *restore*—
serviced herself by a bore, or worse.
What slight of ours brings her chilled,

unremitting gaze? She seems about
          to speak—of what? The look she bares,
her face, has depths that trouble Romer.

Could it be Manet has nothing else
of her than what he shares:
          heavily, she leans on the bar & stares.

CANTO XXX - WORKING OF THE SPHERES

When the Septentrion of the First Heaven...

Romer's cell phone rang in the dream,
as if a collision at distance beyond
reckoning had made connection

through ethereal circuitry to his cell.
It was Ken Belacqua, clear as when
he sat behind Romer at his desk,

centered in the room, calling to him
over others' chatter. Romer took this as
the usual. He had read about the chirp

reaching us from a billion light years away,
the one which rose to the note
of middle C before snapping silent.

They spoke every day this way, as they
interpreted some god-engineer's
ideas, turning them to another's work.

Belacqua's voice had that same crackle
at the glottal edge that ex-drunks have.
Romer asked how he was doing,

remembering his headaches,
the plate in his skull put there
after they dragged him

off Omaha Beach.
Oh fine. Had a good steak
last night, & that Portuguese wine

I like, & met a woman…
Romer realized then he must be dead,
all those years passing since

they had worked together, all that time
waving in the ether between them,
until proof that they lived

at that time, together, in that place,
on the far edge of memory, came
to him over the radiation

of a cell signal, like an echo
that had finally caught him,
racing as he was, through time.

*

A grocery clerk grins
& half-fills his paper bags.
I won't make them heavy—

what cheek she has, sizing him up,
yet Romer lets her carry them to his car.
After her first day at school

their little girl called the hill to home
a *heavy one*, its incline sorrowed
her four-year-old thighs

already weighed by change.
Ego once compelled Romer add more weight.
Heaviness would make him stronger.

When they married, she felt as light
as her trailing veil—
her belief in his strong arm,

how she felt as Romer lifted her to bed—
but then, years had a silent subtraction.
Age wants to go unnoticed,

grinning, awaiting another spring,
much like a withered tree belies
the brittle leanness of its limbs.

It's illusion, bone-heaviness,
a mantle thrown over you one night...
illusion, that your skin thickens to horn.

In reality your skin thins
to soiled tissue, & your bones hollow out.
It's another kind of heaviness.

Steps grow precarious.
Romer sometimes thinks the plod & creak
anneals for things to come,

when gravity no longer matters.
Yet hours with her, lovely moments,
weigh themselves with haste.

Canto XXXI - Hold Tight

"You, standing there, beyond the sacred stream…"

It comes to him, a voice in his sleep.
            More a place of oracles,
whether life or not he cannot tell.

            Close to sleep, he unlaces
to make up the world—
pulls at doors, probes into nests

& lets space around him billow out.
            So much depends on release,
ceding being here & what may follow.

It's well understood by gurus
this recumbent ease, to mind-drift
in wilderness caves—

in tumbled shreds on the millrace.
Close to sleep, Romer notes
shimmers on the darkened glass

& lets them lead him, the many—
            small as they be, trivial, swirled
(but when showering round him,

too slick for thought's grip),
only to be taken & unfurled—
            to make up the world

            as luminous phantasmagoria.
Such happenings fall on a walk
on slumber's edge: slight as

the dervish whirl of a dying wasp,
or a condom boating in a gutter—grave
      as a breeze-shivered palm that crests

beside the street—silent
as an old man, sky-rapt—
vivid as a woman trotting,

her infant bouncing on her breasts.
      Pull at doors, probe into nests,
    the glimpses not truly seen:

a crow-diving jay against
cerulean blue, a spewed sprinkler,
pipeless beside dusty oleanders,

a shredded porno page adhering
      by a thigh to a sewer grate,
a bloody paw-print-trail meandering

the sidewalk—conundrums of a tide,
quick & deep—so, at sleep, he peers about
      & lets space around him billow out.

CANTO XXXII - STRAIGHT INTO THE SUN

I fixed my eyes on her; they were intent...

They left the bus. Others stretched or strolled
or smoked. Grass, a luscious mess, so copious
below a Highland sky, where rolled a cloud,

murk-edged, fluffed, conjoined with violet blues.
The bull, a brilliant *muckle moo* behind
a piled-stone dyke, surveyed what they intended

in stolid Celtic fashion, raised his head
& dripping snout to fingers she extended.
Her arm was bare, so pale against cerul-

ean of her smock. The shaggy head curled free
its meaty tongue as if it felt the pull—
desired like Romer did—to serve as simile.

Her laugh, her folded arms beneath her breasts,
her fingers moving on her belly's plane,
as pregnant women do. Her hair, flame-tressed,

betrayed the bull's. *It's rusted from the rain,*
she said. *Nae body's bairn,* & smiled.
He almost missed that smile, some fumbled snaps.

It's not on film, but found in what's remembered,
the country not attributed to maps,
just at distance down the mountain's side.

*

A fog-lit town at night, Harbor City,
with islands of gold swimming in mist.
Romer found the on-ramp to the Harbor freeway

illumined like a stage's apron,
& entered its arc, its hard right—
a sweep, like a dream's feathered glide.

Barber's *School For Scandal*
pushed his little car in a gust of violins.
Flutes twined his legs,

the misfiring four sang in vibrato.
Romer went fast, or so it seemed,
past tides of silent cars.

To the beat of his heart Romer stamped
on the German, rubber-matted floor.
Note after note, aching & mellow.

Perfection rolled the wheels over tarry,
fretted lanes—measure after measure
fluttering over bibs of concrete.

Back there, in an institutional bed
against an ecru wall, Romer's young wife—
her face leeched by fluorescents—

slept in a muddle of pear-green wraps.
No room they told him. No room but this bed.
The corridor bustled with arms & sheets,

a sump of woman odors. Stark trilling.
Still, swaddled in safety, slept the wee one,
his incredible pinch behind glass.

Canto XXXIII - So High Above

"Deus venerunt gentes, sang the nymphs…"

Oh God, the nations may come, your
        inheritance occupied, but each person
one day wakens, & looks about.

Like coming alert on a train
        after gazing
mesmerized out the window

at scenes you're leaving,
        realizing
that back there—

that expanse of distance & time
        with all its swift banalities—
you forgot & somehow left

a cache of something
        sitting disregarded,
& there ought to be another chance

to hit the ball,
        to catch forty-winks,
to not turn away,

to forget your all-consuming self,
        to properly pack a tube of toothpaste
for the tomorrows—

not peer instead, haplessly,
        at branches racing past
in the darkening.

What measures sustain the choir?
Back they come, the arpeggios
chiming on a Sunday afternoon:

harmonies held forth in heuristic books
from all Romer's desultory sources—
he hears their complacencies of logic

resonate in his walls. His tea grows tepid.
He watches the rug's edge unravel.
So many drowsy hours

thumb-sucking in a sunny chair.
Taunting him, as in a humid tropic,
are gleams of recognition,

faces in a languid queue,
a *dèjá vu* cliché. Romer sorts & rearranges
but fails to grasp connections.

      It remains an unskeined jumble,
a snarl to spindle into threads.
If he pulls a happenstance, knots it cleverly

to focus, perhaps he'll have a *bas-relief*,
emboss some portent from the woof.
He's urged much like a swallow flits—

this way & that, oblique to perpendicular.
It's always the *other way* to others,
as if he could separate himself. He glides,

he thinks, peers through windows, overhears
rumors, watches pretenses in an ordered day.
He leans toward the impetus of any benison.

But *non sequiturs* arise...the dying of a child,
a good woman's agonies...
they fling him into chaos. Fling him.

       The Gobi has no leafy bowers.
Sand whistles there off heraldic bones,
teeth chew beneath arid wadis

amidst dreams of fronds & gutting.
Like skin, blown grit arranges beds
in a texture of expectant folds.

Even stones contain a glint of life,
retain memory, an imprint heel,
an ardent chase through lush glades

in rain, one instant's pass
on the weld of known & new.
A goatherd may wander tracking strays,

may ignite his candle, & out of gloom
will come outlined relics, spinning yet,
flung as the endless tether uncoils.

       Vagary. Mystery. A sea of faces.
Romer supposes he must relent, accept what's dealt.
His fault's an ineptitude of ego,

an all too common failing, disinterest—
Keats surmised that only two
truly gave their utter selves. More exist.

Even now they chant in Lhasa,
risk somewhere a corrective assassination.
Without amanuenses they come & go,

leave their knee prints, wan parings,
& poor, unclaimed duffels—
they thread out like sap, nurture unseen.

He'll never have the chutzpah
to surrender so (or give away his loves,
because he loves them so).

		He observes night's starry flashes.
From the vibrant jungle he hears cries
that penetrate an inscrutable green.

So many, so many dead lay round,
like leaves ripped in winds' elations.
Yet, with sun coiling off petals,

Romer hesitates, feels an urge once more
to reconcile all the disparate voices:
a lapis sky, another's salient cheer,

a flower's complexities, saliva on his tongue...
if this be *an old chaos of the sun*
it still pulls at unseen depths—

unwordable, delving, wrapped
in the placid herbage of ignoble roots
that simply hold....

NOTES:

Each Canto is introduced by the first line of the corresponding Canto in Dante Alighieri's *Purgatorio* (Mark Musa translation).

Canto I: *"I saw the opening maw of hell..."*: from Herman Melville's *Moby Dick*, Chapter 9.

Canto III: On April 30, 1844, Henry David Thoreau started a forest fire in the Concord woods after building a fire in a stump with a friend, "Indian-like," to cook some fish for lunch. It scorched a 300-acre swath, and led to considerable criticism.

Canto VI: A folk belief that going barefoot was a viable cure for colds and rheumatic fever.

Bull Durham was a loose leaf tobacco sold in a draw-stringed cotton pouch until 1988 (now frequently seen for sale on eBay at extortionate prices). The pouch was perfect for marbles.

Canto VII: "Go Directly To Jail" is reference to a penalty in the Parker game of Monopoly.

Canto VIII: Nachash (Hebrew) signifies the serpent of the Tree of Knowledge, the chief villain in Genesis 3:1 of the Bible. The serpent also came and fled in Dante's Canto VIII of *Purgatorio*.

Canto IX: Filippo Brunelleschi (1377-1446) is credited with the first use of linear perspective in art and architectural design (e.g., design of the dome of the Florence Cathedral).

"Let That Be Your Last Battlefield" is the fifteenth episode on the third season of the science fiction television show, *Star Trek*. Frank Gorshin is best known for his role as Bele, who is half black and half white. The sides of Bele's black and white skin are reversed from those of Lokai (Lou Antonio), Bele's mortal enemy. The underlying subject of this episode is slavery and racial segregation.

Canto X: "Blake's Urizen & his calipers..." reference William Blake's complicated mythology. Urizen can mean either "your reason" or a Greek word meaning to limit. Urizen is the embodiment of law and conventional wisdom. He is usually depicted with architect's tools in the act of creating and constraining the universe.

Canto XI: Oral Roberts (1918-2009), an Oklahoma televangelist and charismatic Methodist-Pentecostal, known for his funding appeals.

Canto XIII: young Russian: Vladimir Nabokov in his autobiography, *Speak Memory.*

Canto IXX: Kodacolor: a color film introduced in 1942 by Eastman Kodak, who claimed it "the world's first true color negative film." It was produced until 1963. The color film Kodacolor VT-G400 is still available.

Canto XXI: "Care, whose ravelings Will would knit...": warp of Shakespeare's *Macbeth*, Act 2, Scene 2. Also, in later verses of Canto XXI, is a riff on Philip Larkin's, "Church Going." "Delight and dole" lifted from Shakespeare's *"Hamlet."*

Canto XXIII: "...weld of petals & dough.": reference to Carl Sandburg's definition of poetry as "...the synthesis of hyacinths and biscuits."

Canto XXVI: On his final poetry-reading tour of the United States Dylan Thomas stayed at the Chelsea Hotel, 222 West 23rd, in New York City. He died there October 12, 1978.

Canto XXVII: Salt is harvested at Cuyutlan, Mexico. The salt was originally used by the Spanish in mining and processing silver.

Canto XXIX: Edouard Manet's, "A Bar At The Folies Bergere" (1882).

Canto XXX: The Septentrion constellation is thought to be the Ursa Minor (the Little Dipper).

In February, 2016, scientists announced that they had heard and recorded the sound of two black holes colliding a billion light years away, a fleeting chirp that confirmed the last prediction of Einstein's general theory of relativity.

Canto XXXII: A *muckle moo*, or *heilan coo*, is a Scottish cattle breed originated in the Highlands. The cattle have long horns and long wavy coats that are colored red.

Canto XXXIII: "What measures sustain the choir…": The canto is a riff on Wallace Stevens', "Sunday Morning."

ABOUT THE AUTHOR

Robert Eastwood is a prize-winning poet who lives in San Ramon, California. He has been published widely, online and in print. His previous book, *Snare*, was published by Broadstone Books in 2016. He welcomes comments or questions at boble38@sbcglobal.net.

Books from Etruscan Press

Human Directional | Diane Raptosh

Saint Joe's Passion | JD Schraffenberger

Lies Will Take You Somewhere | Sheila Schwartz

Fast Animal | Tim Seibles

One Turn Around the Sun | Tim Seibles

Rough Ground | Alix Anne Shaw

A Heaven Wrought of Iron: Poems From the Odyssey | D. M. Spitzer

American Fugue | Alexis Stamatis

The Casanova Chronicles | Myrna Stone

Luz Bones | Myrna Stone

In the Cemetery of the Orange Trees | Jeff Talarigo

The White Horse: A Colombian Journey | Diane Thiel

The Arsonist's Song Has Nothing to Do With Fire | Allison Titus

The Fugitive Self | John Wheatcroft

YOU. | Joseph P. Wood

ETRUSCAN PRESS IS PROUD OF SUPPORT RECEIVED FROM

Wilkes University

Youngstown State University

The Raymond John Wean Foundation

The Ohio Arts Council

The Stephen & Jeryl Oristaglio Foundation

The Nathalie & James Andrews Foundation

The National Endowment for the Arts

The Ruth H. Beecher Foundation

The Bates-Manzano Fund

The New Mexico Community Foundation

Founded in 2001 with a generous grant from the Oristaglio Foundation, Etruscan Press is a nonprofit cooperative of poets and writers working to produce and promote books that nurture the dialogue among genres, achieve a distinctive voice, and reshape the literary and cultural histories of which we are a part.

etruscan press

www.etruscanpress.org

Etruscan Press books may be ordered from

Consortium Book Sales and Distribution

800.283.3572

www.cbsd.com

Etruscan Press is a 501(c)(3) nonprofit organization.
Contributions to Etruscan Press are tax deductible
as allowed under applicable law.
For more information, a prospectus,
or to order one of our titles,
contact us at books@etruscanpress.org.